Whether as a backdrop or centre-stage, New Zealand's stunning scenery played a vital role in the transformation of J.R.R. Tolkien's fantasy epic into the multiple-award-winning film trilogy, *The Lord of the Rings*. The drama, majesty and breathtaking beauty of the land's varied forms made New Zealand first-choice location for the movies, and allowed it to become, for three years of filming at least, the realm of Middle-earth.

While the films portrayed a fantasy world, the scenery was real. The movie trilogy offered tantalising glimpses, but there is a lot more to see and savour. New Zealand's natural wonders encompass the wild and the serene, spanning everything from snowcapped peaks to golden beaches, with lush forest and fertile farmland in between. Reflecting the country's diversity, this collection of images follows three broad themes.

Snow, fire and ice represents some of the country's most dramatic and spectacular landforms, still in the process of creation. The mountain spine of both islands is being thrust upwards as tectonic plates clash, while glaciers and fiords bear witness to the power of the snow and ice that descend from them. Plate collision also fuels active volcanoes and geothermal activity in the heart of the North Island.

Forest, hills and water shows that New Zealand's plentiful rain and snow provide water for innumerable streams, rivers and lakes. As well as being clothed in a mantle of rolling hills, pastureland and plains, over a third of the country remains forested.

Sand, surf and sea depicts some of New Zealand's long and varied coastline, with rocky shores and sandy beaches, tranquil bays, quiet coves or wave-lashed headlands.

Here is some of New Zealand's varied colour, beauty and mystery: the startling shapes of clouds over alpine lakes, moss-draped goblin glades, tide-patterned golden sands and foaming seas. Welcome to the unique world of the real Middle-earth.

SNOW, FIRE AND ICE ARE SOME OF THE FORCES THAT HAVE CREATED NEW ZEALAND'S SPECTACULAR LANDSCAPES AND CONTINUE TO REMODEL IT. THE COUNTRY IS CAUGHT IN THE ZONE BETWEEN THE AUSTRALIAN AND THE PACIFIC CRUSTAL PLATES. THE COLLISION PUSHES UP THE THE SOUTHERN ALPS AND THE NORTH ISLAND RANGES, WHILE ALSO FUELLING THE TAUPO VOLCANIC ZONE IN THE CENTRAL NORTH ISLAND.

Previous pages: A new day dawns over snow-clad Mt Freyberg and a partly frozen tarn in Lewis Pass National Reserve, Canterbury.

The Taupo Volcanic Zone extends from White Island in the Bay of Plenty to the volcanoes of the Tongariro National Park. Mt Ngauruhoe (**opposite** and **above**) is the youngest and most frequently active of the volcanoes.

Left: The Taupo Volcanic Zone encompasses the Whakarewarewa Thermal Reserve in Rotorua, an other-worldly landscape of hot springs, mud pools, fumaroles and thundering geysers, such as the famous Pohutu, which throws out its superheated steam some 30 metres high.

Previous pages: The Rotorua-Taupo district features many geothermal areas. At Waiotapu Thermal Reserve, the Artist's Palette, incorporating the Champagne Pool bubbling with escaping gas, is a vivid spectrum of colour created by mineral-rich water.

Left: The South Island's alps have been pushed up in the collision of crustal plates, and are still rising a metre every century, although erosion keeps their height trimmed. In South Canterbury, tussocklands sweep up to Red Mountain in the Rangitata Valley.

Opposite below: The Mid Canterbury high country features sheep farms located amid what early surveyor Charles Torlesse described as 'a romantic and chaotic mass of mountains'. Here Castle Hill Station lies before the Torlesse Range.

Below: Sheep graze in the looming presence of Purple Hill at Flock Hill Station in the Mid Canterbury high country.

Above: Canterbury features several lakes in stunning alpine settings. In Mid Canterbury, a serene Lake Tyler reflects the snow-covered Mt Hutt.

Left: The South Island's mountains feed numerous glaciers and countless streams. The Lewis River rushes past the Libretto Range near Lewis Pass, its water eventually joining the great, braided shingle river of the Waiau, flowing across North Canterbury.

Opposite: Lake Camp in South Canterbury, frozen in mid-winter ice.

Left: Ice has left its mark on New Zealand, as glaciers have advanced or retreated, depending on the climate, gouging out mountains and depositing sediments. Some of the largest remaining are the Fox, Franz Josef, and Tasman glaciers. In Westland/Tai Poutini National Park, Small Kettle Lake was formed by the retreating Fox Glacier, now in a period of advancement. Some 13 kilometres long, the river of ice descends steeply from 2750 metres above sea level to 245 metres.

Above: Franz Josef Glacier in Westland/Tai Poutini National Park, seen from near the Sentinel Rock lookout, is now advancing at an average rate of a metre a day after a long period of retreat.

Opposite top: Early morning mist rises off bush-fringed Lake Matheson near Fox Glacier township in Westland/Tai Poutini National Park. The waters provide perfect reflections of the Southern Alps' highest peaks of Aoraki/Mt Cook (3754 m) and Mt Tasman (3497 m).

Opposite lower: A frozen alpine tarn before Mt Dome in Arthur's Pass National Park.

Above: Aoraki/Mt Cook looks over Lake Pukaki. Snow from the mountain feeds the Tasman Glacier and then Tasman River before flowing into the lake. The water contains suspended particles of rock, finely ground by the glacier, which gives the lake its characteristic pale blue hue.

Previous pages: The country's highest peak, Aoraki/Mt Cook is framed by the hills of the Hooker Valley, through which flow the glacier-fed waters of the Hooker River in Aoraki/Mt Cook National Park.

Left: In the Hooker Valley is one of the most popular walks in the Aoraki/Mt Cook National Park. Here a tramper crosses the swing bridge over the Hooker River, with Mt Sefton in the background.

Below: The still waters of Milford Sound reflect Mt Phillips at left with the 1695-metre Mitre Peak in the centre. Carved out by ice-age glaciers, the fiord winds its way 22 kilometres to the Tasman Sea, and its high walls plunge sheer into the inky waters.

Opposite: Blue Lake, usually more green than blue, sits before the hulk of Mt Wakefield in Aoraki/Mt Cook National Park.

In the south-west of the South Island, Fiordland National Park in the Te Wahi Pounamu World Heritage Area is a magnificent, pristine wilderness of mountains, forest and fiords. In the Hollyford Valley, Lake Marion (**left**) mirrors Mt Crosscut. The spectacular steep-sided trapezium of Mitre Peak (**below**), seen rising beyond the Cleddau River, has become the symbol of Milford Sound and is typical of Fiordland's many dramatic granite peaks.

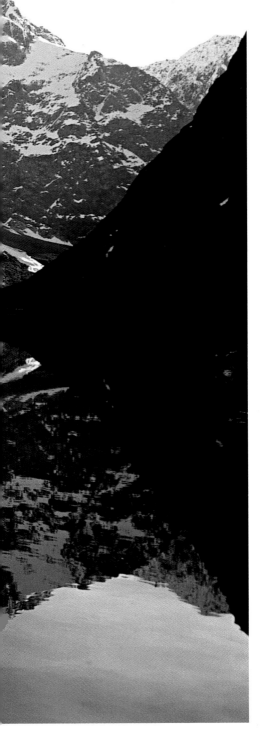

NEW ZEALAND IS SUPERBLY GREEN.
ABUNDANT SNOW AND RAIN FEED RIVERS,
FALLS, LAKES, LAGOONS AND SWAMPLANDS.
AROUND A QUARTER OF THE COUNTRY
REMAINS CLOAKED IN UNIQUE AND DIVERSE
FORESTS, MOST PROTECTED IN PARKS AND
RESERVES. ROLLING HILLS AND LUSH LOWLAND
PASTURES ARE ALSO ESSENTIAL ELEMENTS OF
THE SCENERY.

Previous pages: The brilliantly coloured
Maruia River flows through a narrow
gorge near Maruia Springs in Westland.

Mangapohue Stream (**above**) meanders
near Waitomo in the central North
Island, the site of various limestone cave
complexes featuring caverns, 'black-
water' rivers, glow-worms, stalactites
and stalagmites, such as in Aranui Cave
(**left**) at the Ruakuri Scenic Reserve.

Volcanic activity helped create most of
the North Island's large lakes, with Lake
Taupo (**opposite top**) filling the
depression created by a huge caldera.
The Waikato River, the country's
longest, forms the outlet to Lake Taupo.
Not far from the lake, the river spills
through a narrow chasm in a fury of
foam over Huka Falls (**opposite lower**).

Top: Lush farmland south of Te Kuiti in the North Island's King Country. Dairying dominates in the North Island's fertile regions of the Waikato, Bay of Plenty and Taranaki, while hillier country usually carries sheep.

Above: Snow and a high rainfall mean numerous streams and major rivers, including the Waikato and Whanganui, begin on the slopes of the central North Island's volcanoes. Tawhai Falls grace the lower slopes of Mt Ruapehu.

Opposite: Bush and fern-edged, Pukeiti Stream descends through the magical setting of rainforest on the slopes of Taranaki/Mt Egmont in Egmont National Park.

Previous pages: The dormant cone of Taranaki/Mt Egmont sits alone in the west of the North Island, its slopes carpeted with forest, including the dim, moss-draped 'goblin forest', a testament to the high rainfall, up to 7500 millimetres per year in some places, which provides a profusion of watercourses and a myriad mosses, lichens and ferns.

Opposite: Tree ferns, of which New Zealand has a wealth of species, thrive alongside the Torrent River, near Torrent Bay in the South Island's Abel Tasman National Park.

Above: A gnarled tree trunk and moss-covered boulder create an eerie composition in the Bealey Valley in Arthur's Pass National Park, South Island.

Right: The ethereal Mossy Creek Falls are typical of those on bush-covered streams of Arthur's Pass National Park.

Left: Sunflowers in full bloom carpet a field in the patchwork of pasture and cropland of the Canterbury Plains, with the Mt Hutt Range in the distance.

Below: The warm colours of autumn willows and waving plumes of toetoe, the largest native grass, contrast with the cool solidity of Mt Dome in Arthur's Pass National Park. Arthur's Pass provides the highest and most spectacular road crossing of the Southern Alps, an area of glacier-gouged valleys between scree-covered mountains and wide shingle riverbeds.

In the Mid Canterbury high country, a perfectly still Lake Pearson (**opposite top**) reflects willow trees and the Torlesse Range. Lake Pearson, typical of the small shallow lakes in the area, is almost two lakes, as it narrows severely in the centre. The stark peaks of the Torlesse Range (**opposite lower**) seem to float above autumn mists in the Craigieburn Valley.

Opposite top: Morning mist rises off Lake Paringa, north of Haast in South Westland. Remoteness, groaning glaciers grinding down almost to sea level, primaeval pristine rainforest, serene lakes and rapid rain-fed rivers all help make the South Island's West Coast a place of wonder and sublime beauty.

Opposite lower: Coal Creek Falls, near Greymouth in Westland. The West Coast is wet: a torrential rainfall sees streams and rivers rushing off the hills to the sea.

Above: Morning mist and mirror-like stillness accentuate the superlative, unspoiled beauty of Lake Kaniere, near Hokitika in Westland.

Left: The West Coast's farms, like this one near Fox Glacier township, sit on a narrow strip of land between the Tasman Sea and the Southern Alps.

Opposite: In Westland/Tai Poutini National Park, kahikatea trees stand with their feet in the still waters of Lake Wahapo. Kahikatea, common in lowland forests, are the tallest native tree and often the dominant species in swampy bushland and moist alluvial flats.

Sunlight illuminates reeds and forest alongside the Kohaihai River in Kahurangi National Park (**above**). The park encompasses a wide range of forest and mountain areas in the north-west of the South Island. At Karamea on the coastal fringe of the park (**right**), stately nikau, New Zealand's only native palm, luxuriate in the area's warmer climate.

Mount Aspiring National Park covers a rugged region in the South Island's south-west, straddling the Southern Alps, and offers fine walking tracks. In its higher regions are icy peaks, deep glacial valleys and over 100 glaciers. The wetter western side supports dense forest, rich in ferns and mosses. Robinsons Creek (**above**) flows near Haast Pass in the north of the park. The southern region of the park features moody beech forest, such as that alongside the Routeburn Track (**opposite**), its lighter canopy allowing a carpet of mosses to grow.

Left: The Mclean River is one of many gentle bush-shrouded streams in the Catlins Forest Park. The park, alongside the South Island's southern coast, offers a remarkable variety of scenery that includes rainforest, rivers, lakes and waterfalls, rocky shores and sandy beaches.

Left: Rainfall in Mount Aspiring National Park is heavy. The magical Blue River flows near Haast Pass.

Below: Enormous slabs of schist form the foundation of the Haast River, which runs through bushland before entering a wide valley on its way to the sea.

Central Otago is a majestic wide inland plateau of tussock-clad rounded hills dramatised by a constantly changing interplay of light and shadow, bare lonely plains and deep glacial lakes flanked by steeply rising ranges. The tussock high country of Lindis Pass (**opposite top**) is typical of the region.

Opposite lower: Early morning light plays on Skippers Saddle and the Remarkables Range, near Queenstown.

Above: Willow trees in Lake Wanaka with Mt Albert beyond. Introduced species are virtually the only trees in Central Otago, colouring spectacularly in autumn.

Right: Sunrise on the Harris Range and Lake Wanaka.

SAND, SURF AND SEA SURROUND NEW ZEALAND AND THE LONG COASTLINE HAS A MYRIAD VARIATIONS. BAYS, BEACHES, HARBOURS, ESTUARIES, COVES AND HEADLANDS PROVIDE CONSTANTLY CHANGING PANORAMAS.

Previous pages: The impressively sculptural Archway Islands at Whakariki Beach, near Farewell Spit on the north-western tip of the South Island.

Northland's beautiful coastline embraces aquamarine seas, island-studded bays, vast stretches of sand, mangrove-lined harbours and rocky coast. Cape Brett headland (**above**) forms the eastern boundary of the Bay of Islands. The pohutukawa tree (**right**), clinging to the shore at Bland Bay, brightens North Island coasts in a summer blaze of crimson. Maitai Bay (**opposite top**) draws a perfect arc of sand, while pohutukawa frame rocky South Whangaruru Bay (**opposite lower**).

The Coromandel Peninsula features some of the North Island's most stunning scenery, with an indented coastline of bays, beaches, islets and islands. Wind and tide have carved the soft sandstone in Cathedral Cove into stacks such as Te Hoho Rock (**opposite**) and low caverns (**above**). The exquisite Lonely Bay (**left**) is a Coromandel gem.

The Coromandel Peninsula is endowed with many sheltered harbours, such as Whitianga Harbour (**left**) and quiet estuaries, like Purangi Estuary (**opposite top**).

Along the North Taranaki coast near Tongaporutu the sea has fashioned unusual shapes from the sandstone (**below**), including the landmark pillars of the Three Sisters (**opposite lower**). Storms have recently reduced the size of the smallest sister.

Previous pages: The Wairarapa coastline in the south-east of the North Island is a desolate stretch of surf-lashed cliffs and cold seas. At Castlepoint, a reef of tilted rock has created a sheltered lagoon.

The top of the South Island is a maze of waterways in the Marlborough Sounds, and to the west the bush-covered granite hills of Abel Tasman National Park reach down to the waterline and beaches, such as the golden sweep of Totaranui (**left**). Around the north-western tip of the island, wilder seas foam up on Scotts Beach in Kahurangi National Park (**above**).

Above: The sand dunes and islets of Whakariki Beach offer a superb introduction to the South Island's wild and empty West Coast. The beach is reached from Puponga at the base of 26-kilometre-long Farewell Spit, an arc of dunes, shell banks and wetlands that provides an important bird sanctuary.

The rockbound east coast south of Marlborough sits at the edge of a low plain backed by hills and towering mountains. Cape Campbell Lighthouse looks over Clifford Bay (**left**), while the snow-covered Seaward Kaikoura Range provides a perfect backdrop to the Kaikoura Peninsula (**opposite** and **following pages**) with its wave-washed reefs and swaying kelp. Close to the coastline, sperm, humpback and southern right whales can be viewed as they migrate through these waters.

On the West Coast, stony, driftwood-strewn beaches are flanked by forested hills running up to the Southern Alps. The Tasman Sea pounds in relentlessly, making the coast a place of tremendous drama, energy and beauty. At Greigs Beach (**above**), rock pools line the bay below Mt St Patrick, while Jackson Bay, south of Haast (**opposite top**), enjoys the superb backdrop of the Southern Alps.

Opposite lower: Sea water erupts through a blowhole in the limestone layers of Pancake Rocks, a coastal landmark at Punakaiki in the Paparoa National Park.

Above: The sun sets sea cliffs aglow at Truman Bay in the West Coast's Paparoa National Park.

The Otago coastline in the south-east and south of the South Island offers amazing contrasts: tall rocky cliffs, sandy beaches fringing luxuriant forest, placid estuaries and wild, kelp-strewn rocky shores lashed by the Southern Ocean. Taiaroa Head Lighthouse (**left**) sits atop cliffs at the mouth of Otago Peninsula. Royal albatrosses breed here and launch themselves from the rocky heights. At Moeraki Beach (**opposite top**), south of Oamaru, spherical boulders are scattered about like a giant's marbles. Some of the rocks, which eroded out of shoreline bluffs, contain fossilised dinosaur bones.

Opposite lower: On the Catlins Coast in South Otago toetoe wave in the breeze alongside the Purakaunui River at Purakaunui Bay.

Following page: Like stepping stones into the Southern Ocean, the jagged islets, which early whalers called nuggets, give Nugget Point its name.

First published in 2004 by New Holland Publishers (NZ) Ltd
Auckland • Sydney • London • Cape Town

218 Lake Road, Northcote, Auckland, New Zealand
Unit 1, 66 Gibbes Street, Chatswood, NSW 2067, Australia
86–88 Edgware Road, London W2 2EA, United Kingdom
80 McKenzie Street, Cape Town 8001, South Africa

www.newhollandpublishers.co.nz

Copyright © 2004 in photography: Andrew Fear/andrewfear@paradise.net.nz
Copyright © 2004 in text: Brian O'Flaherty
Copyright © 2004 New Holland Publishers (NZ) Ltd

New Zealand edition:
ISBN: 978-1-86966-059-8
United Kingdom edition:
ISBN: 978-1-84330-918-5

Managing editor: Matt Turner
Design: Julie McDermid

A catalogue record for this book is available from the National Library of New Zealand.

5 7 9 10 8 6

Colour reproduction by SC (Sang Choy) International, Singapore
Printed in China through Colorcraft Ltd, Hong Kong

Front cover: The rocky shoreline of Hooker Lake, fed by the Hooker Glacier, with Aoraki/Mt Cook in the background, Aoraki/Mt Cook National Park.
Rear cover: (top) Maori Lake reflects the Taylor Range in the South Canterbury high country; **(lower left)** Stewarts Creek waterfall in Makarora Valley, Mt Aspiring National Park; **(lower right)** Marahau Beach in Abel Tasman National Park.
Introduction page (from left to right): Hooker Lake and Aoraki/Mt Cook; a vine and moss-covered tree trunk near Lake Marion in the Hollyford Valley of Fiordland National Park; low tide sand patterns in the beach at Castlepoint, Wairarapa.